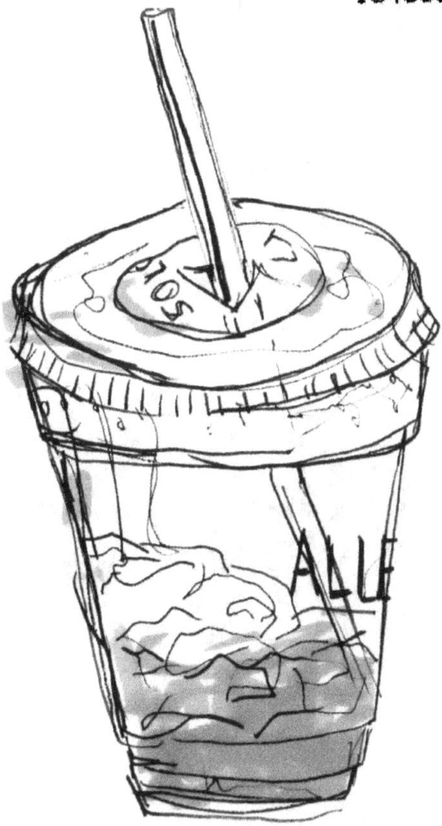
ALLE

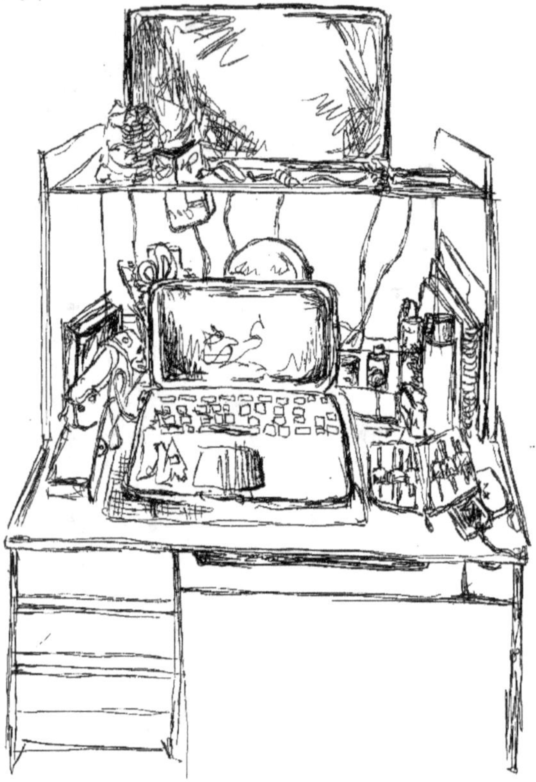

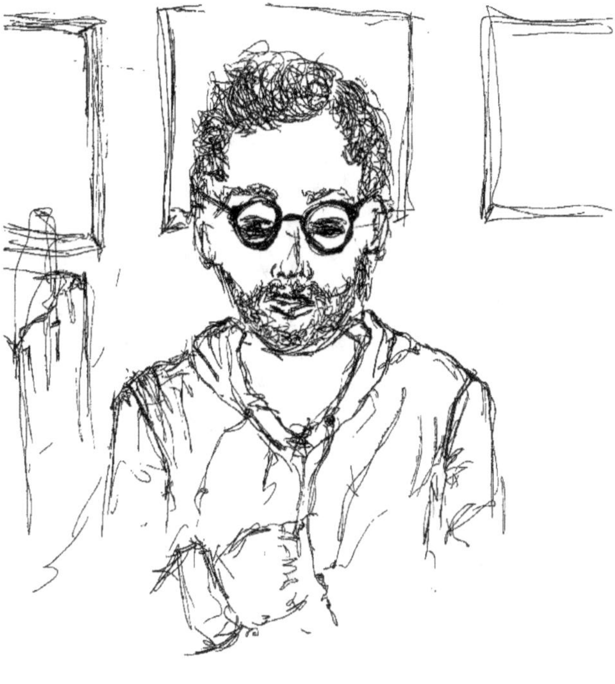

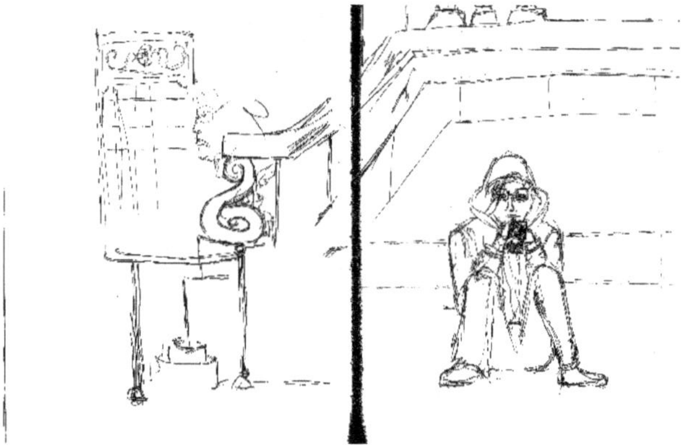

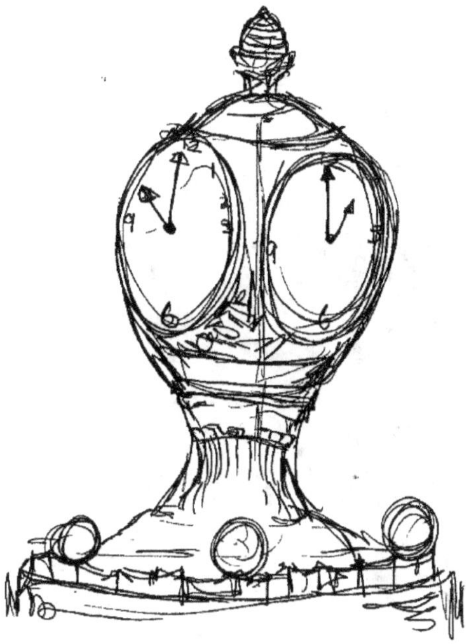

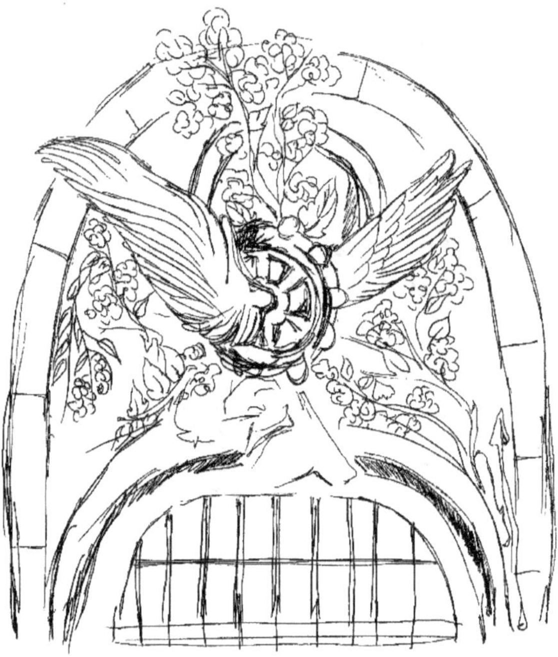

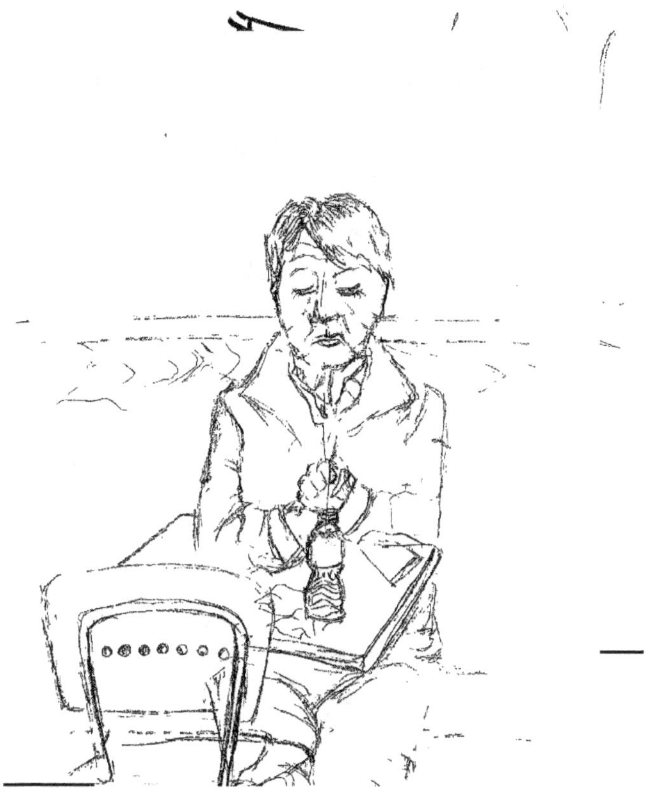

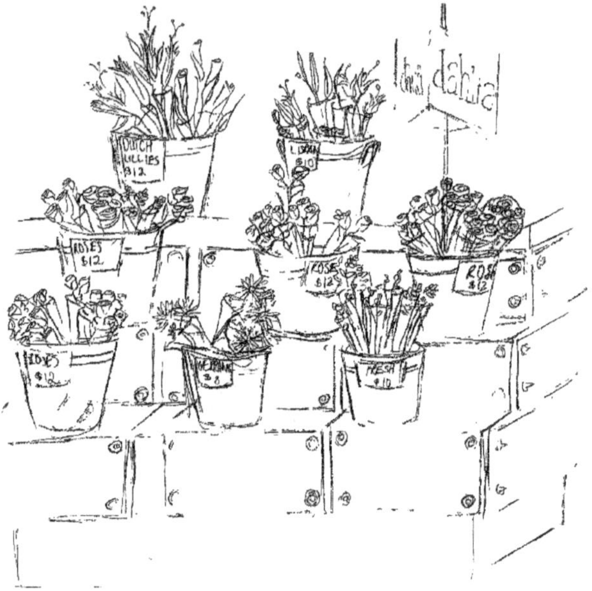
DUTCH LILLIES $12
ROSES $12
FRESH $10

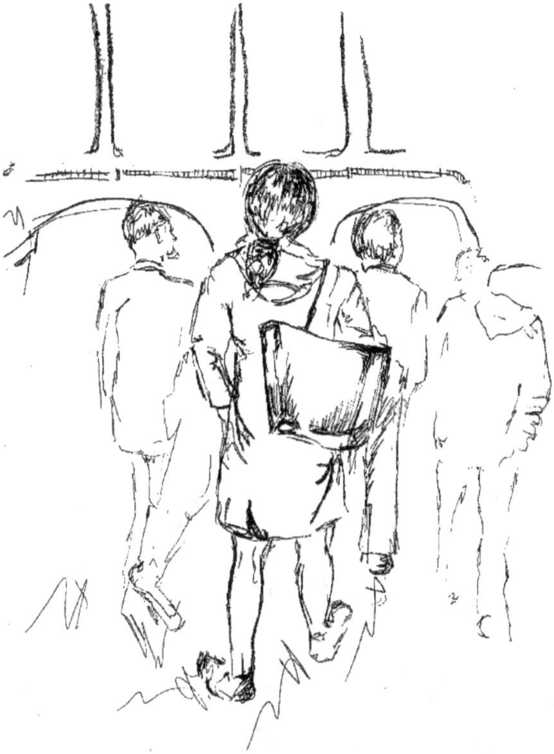

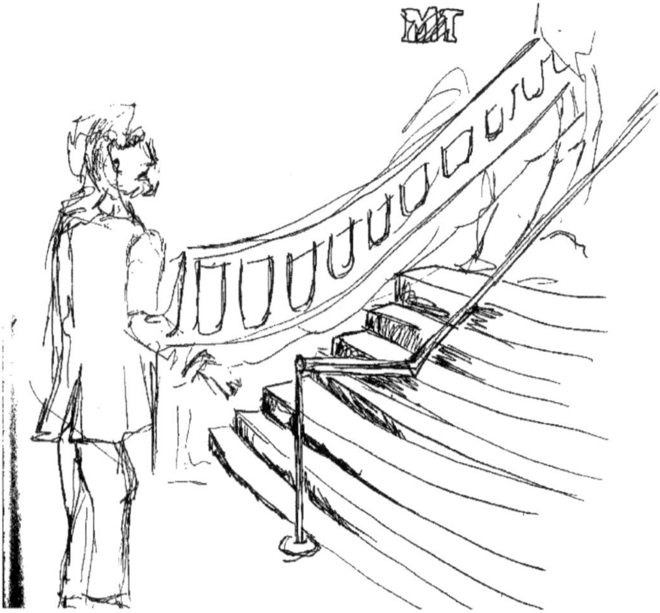
MT

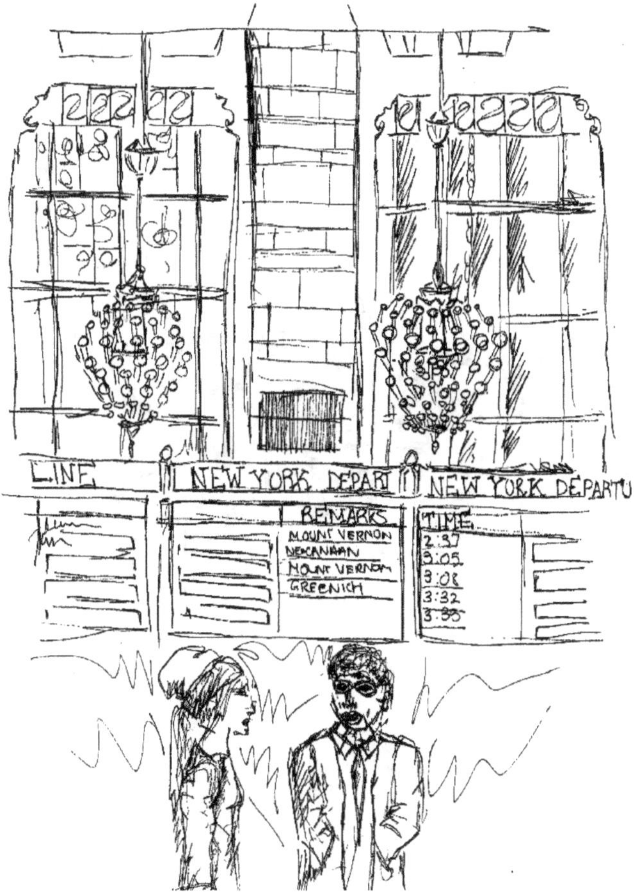
LINE
NEW YORK DEPART
NEW YORK DEPARTU
REMARKS
MOUNT VERNON
NEW CANAAN
MOUNT VERNON
GREENICH
TIME
2:37
3:05
3:08
3:32
3:35

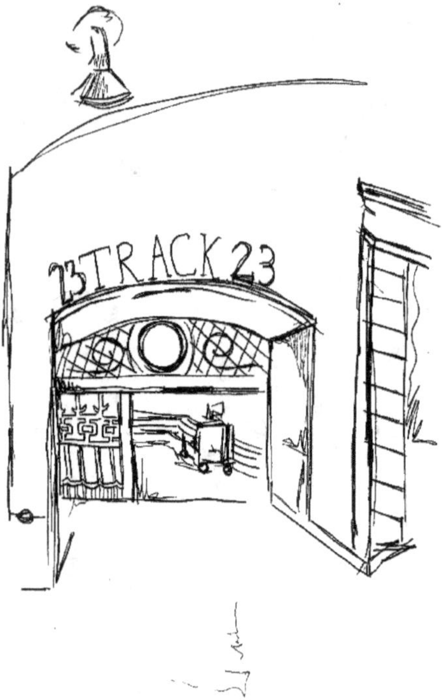
23TRACK 23

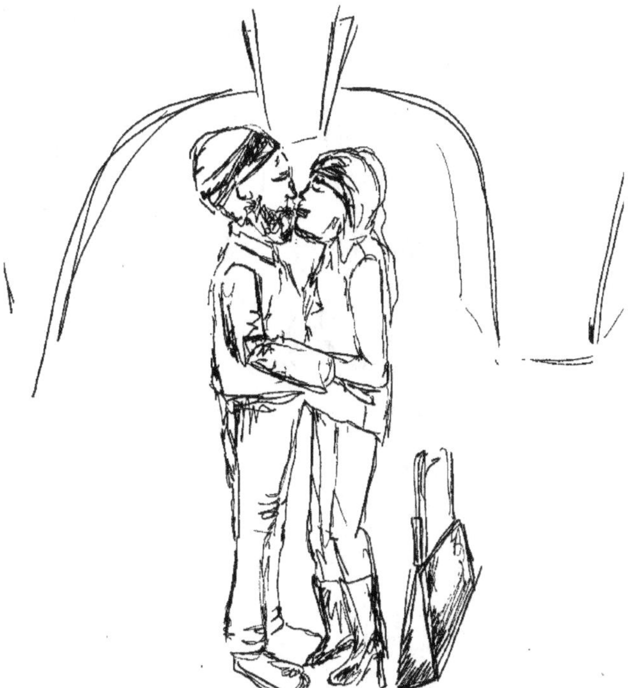

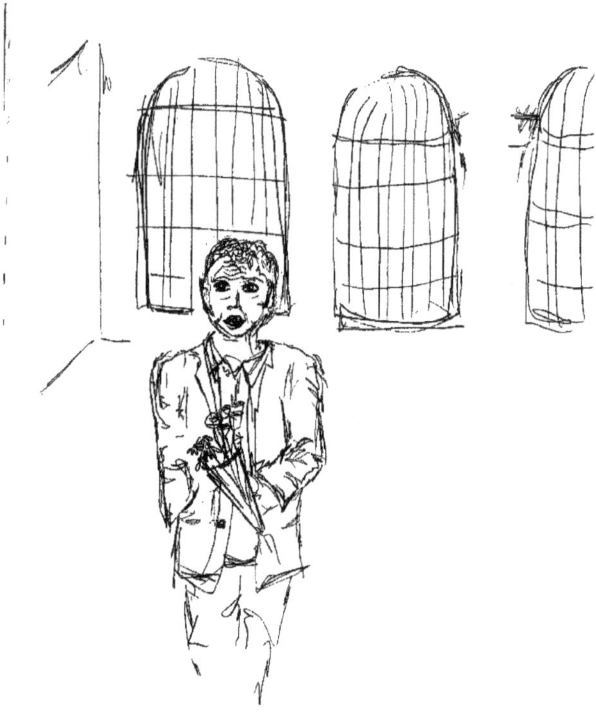

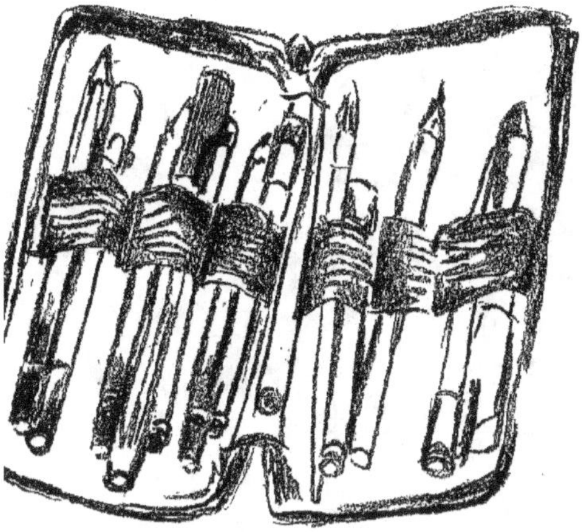

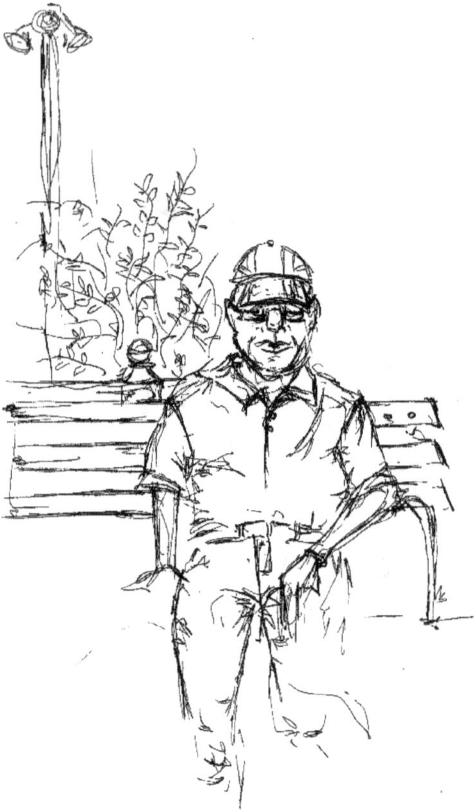

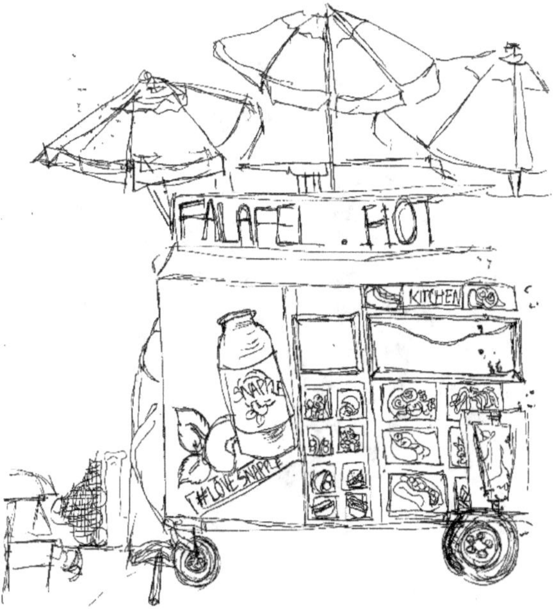
FALAFEL . HOT
KITCHEN
SNAPPLE
#LOVESNAPPLE

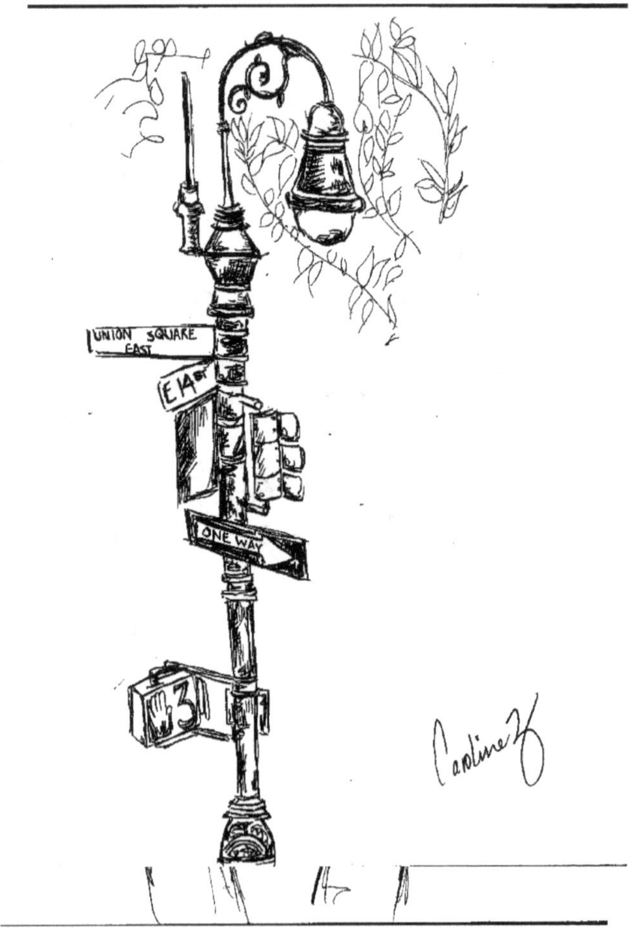
UNION SQUARE
EAST
E 14 ST
ONE WAY
3

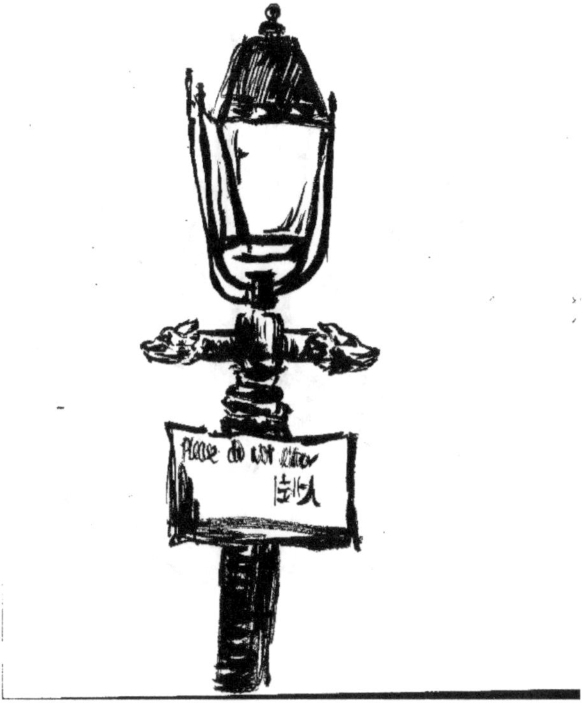
please do not litter

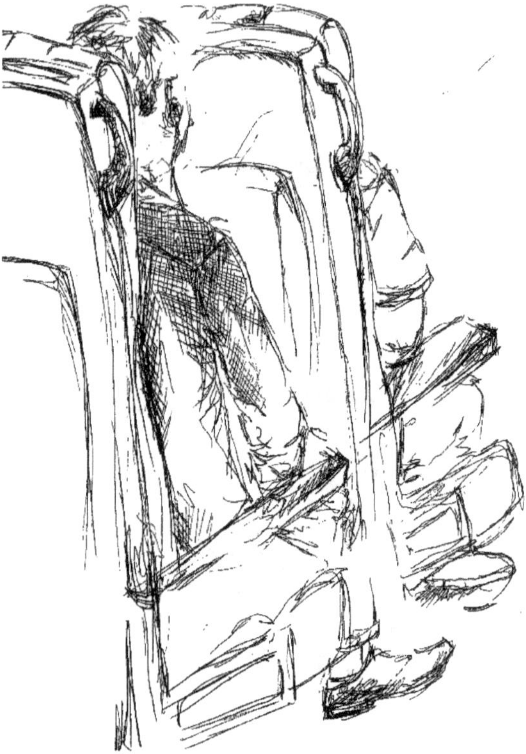

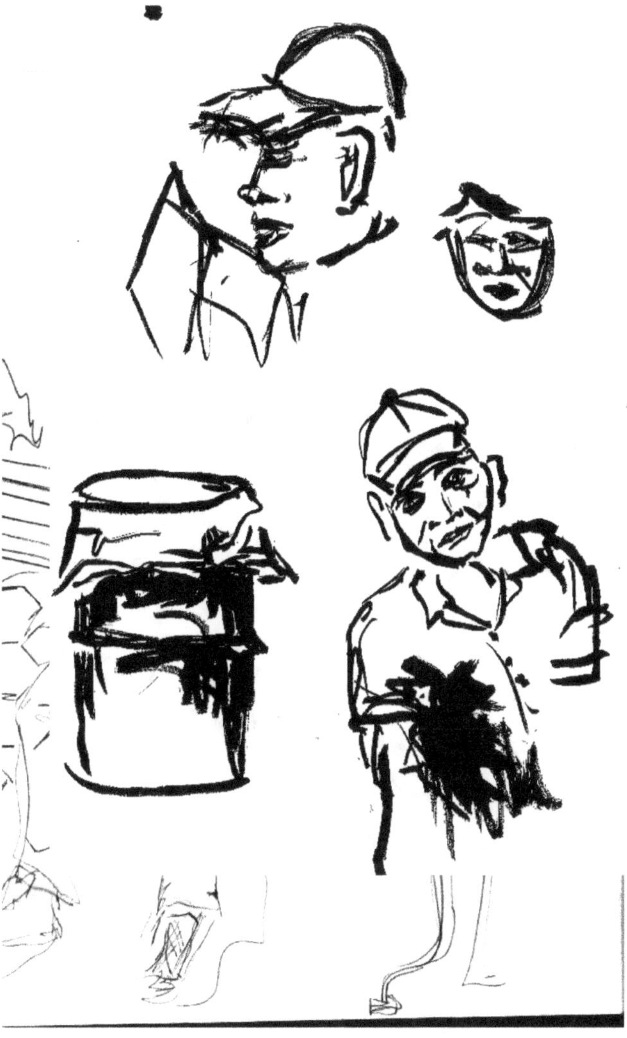

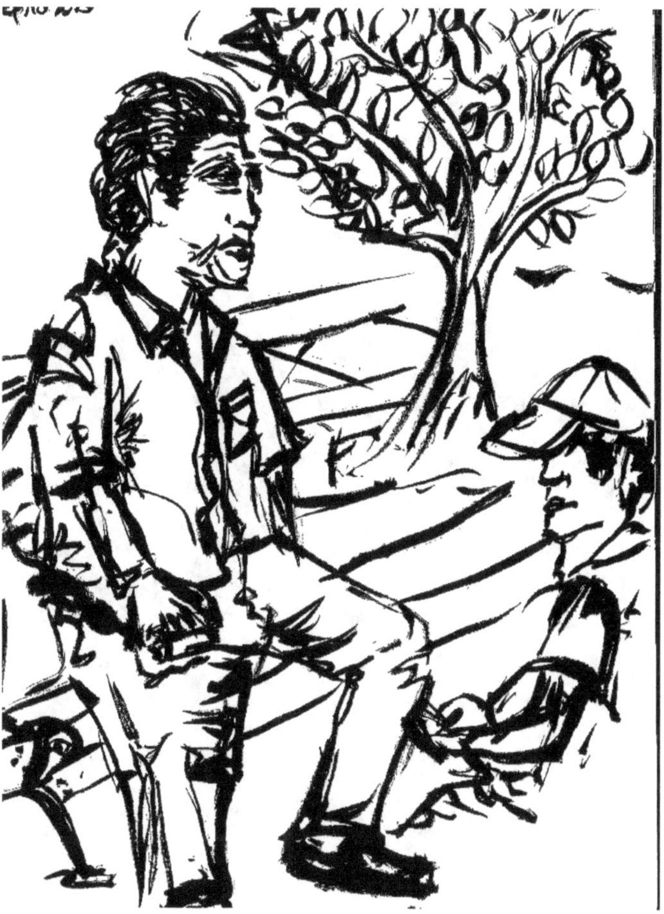

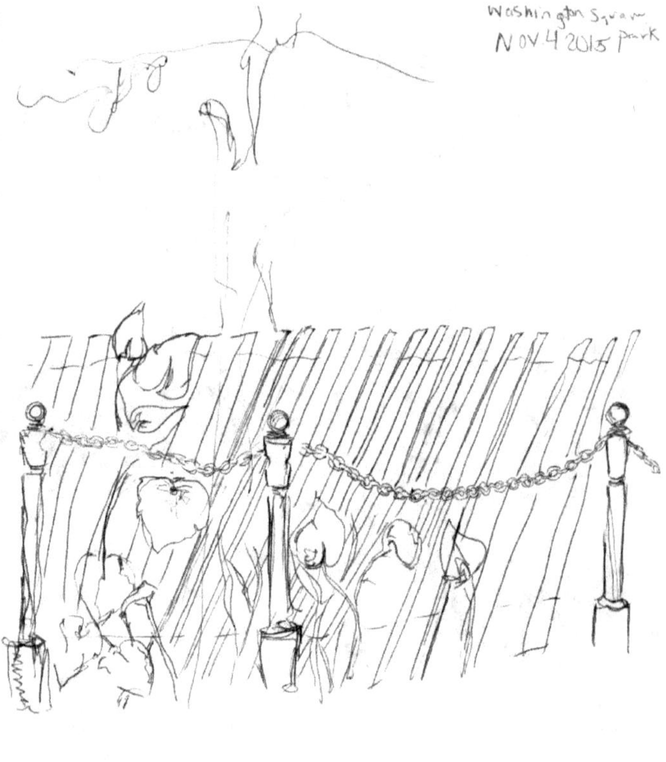
Washington Square Park
NOV 4 2015

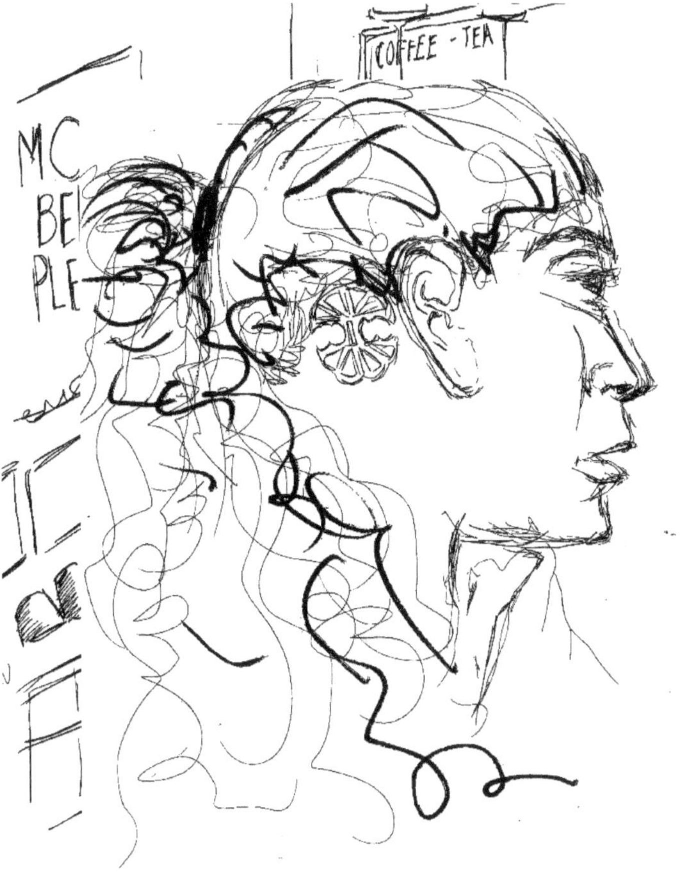
COFFEE - TEA
MC
BE
PLE

www.ingramcontent.com/pod-product-compliance
Lightning Source LLC
Chambersburg PA
CBHW072252200526
45168CB00015B/1709
* 9 7 8 1 5 1 9 1 3 4 4 9 3 *